SUNDAY MONDAY
faith in the World

*Linking Faith on a Sunday
and Life on a Monday*

Six Sessions for Groups

Chris Powell
Wendy S Robins
Christine Allen
David Durston

Scripture Union
130 City Road, London EC1V 2NJ

CASSELL
Wellington House, 125 Strand
London WC2R 0BB

Cassell
Wellington House, 125 Strand, London WC2R 0BB

Scripture Union
130 City Road, London EC1V 2NJ

© 1995 Chris Powell, Wendy S Robins, Christine Allen & David Durston

First published 1995

All Bible quotations in this publication are from the Holy Bible, New Revised Standard Version, copyright © 1989 by the Division of Christian Education of the National Council of the Churches of Christ in the USA and are used by permission.

British Library Cataloguing-in-Publication Data.
A catalogue record for this book is available from the British Library.

ISBN 0 86201 986 9 (*Ten pack* 0 304 33189 9; *Resources book* 0 86201 987 7)

Cover design, illustration and book design by Ross Advertising & Design Ltd, Chesham.
Cartoons by Taffy Davies.
Typeset by Ross Advertising & Design Ltd, Chesham.
Printed and bound in Great Britain by Ebenezer Baylis & Son Ltd, Worcester.

Contents

Introduction

WHAT THIS BOOK IS ABOUT AND HOW IT WORKS

The aim of this series of meetings is to help you explore and develop the links between your faith and your everyday life. Many of us find it hard to take faith out beyond the church doors on a Sunday and into the rest of our lives on a Monday. These meetings give you the chance to:

- think about your experience of everyday life
- make sense of that experience by talking with others and examining the Bible together

- look ahead to develop the ways in which you live out your faith.

The worlds we live in

Each of us is unique - we may be old or young, live alone or with others, be female or male, paid or unpaid for our work - and although we all live on the same planet, we each live and move in our own worlds of home, school, workplace, church and so on. The starting place for this course is you - who you are and the different worlds you live and move and work in. The Bible also begins with you.

Being creative or destructive

The Bible describes God creating the world. People are made in the image of God the creator; we can also be creative. We can take the materials of the created world and make new things from them: food, clothes, homes, art, technology. This is what the annual Harvest festivals, found in almost every culture and religion, celebrate. Building relationships with others is part of this creativity.

Chapter one of Genesis tells us that God gives people 'dominion' over the world. We are to have authority over the world and be responsible for it. We are to live creatively not destructively and be part of making the world the kind of place God intended it to be.

Called to be saints *(Romans 1:7)*

It is good to explore these issues in a group because groups are at the heart of the Bible. There is the group of the Trinity of God; the nation of Israel; the group of disciples; and the group of believers - the church - where the individual experiences being part of the people of God. These groups of individuals, each serving God in their own way, and together forming the church, can be celebrated at the end of this course at the Festival of All Saints or at another special gathering.

INTRODUCTION

THE SESSIONS

This book begins with a meeting that looks at what it is to be you, what it is to be a human being, and the different worlds you and others move in. The second meeting looks at how God wants the whole world, and your individual worlds, to be. The next three meetings look at three main areas of life: work, family, and the local neighbourhood. The last meeting focuses on what it means to be the people of God, the community of God's 'new creation', the church.

Using this book

The material for each meeting contains a number of options. The group leader or some or all of the group members must plan and prepare the meetings in advance. As you decide on the suitability of different activities, keep in mind the background and abilities of the whole group. Different people learn in different ways, and people will be most likely to learn if they feel comfortable and confident in a group. Sometimes a new approach will be helpful in moving people on from present ways of thinking and feeling. Try to strike a balance between choosing activities which use familiar and easy methods and those which seem new or more challenging to you.

There are further ideas about how to set up, plan and lead these group meetings in the resources book.

HOW THE MEETINGS WORK

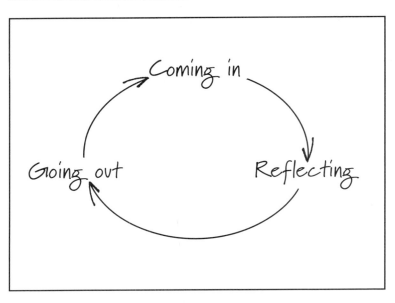

Coming in

You come into the meetings bringing your experience and your worlds into the group.

Reflecting

Then together the group reflects and spends time looking at the Bible and how it connects with individuals and their lives.

Going out

The last part of the meeting is about going out and taking what you have learned into your life in the world.

THE MENU

The menus for meetings give you a choice of different activities. Do not try to do them all. Choose one or more items from each section.

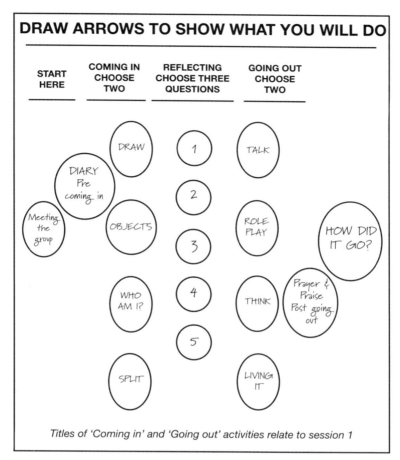

DRAW ARROWS TO SHOW WHAT YOU WILL DO

| START HERE | COMING IN CHOOSE TWO | REFLECTING CHOOSE THREE QUESTIONS | GOING OUT CHOOSE TWO |

Titles of 'Coming in' and 'Going out' activities relate to session 1

The diary

After the first meeting you will be asked to keep a record of certain things you experience in the coming week and in the weeks that follow. The record can be in the form of a written diary, drawings, an audio or video recording - anything that will help you remember what happens during the week. There will be an opportunity at the beginning of every meeting to talk about the previous week. You won't be asked to show others your record, but keeping it will help you remember significant points.

Coming in

Choose two of the activities in this section to help you bring your everyday experience into the group with you.

Reflecting

After reading the Bible passage choose three questions to help you explore what the Bible might have to say about your life and your worlds.

Going out

Choose two of the activities in this section to help you take what you have been thinking and learning back into your worlds.

Prayer and praise

You may want to spend time at the end of the meeting in prayer and praise. Suggestions for this are in the separate resources book.

In the group

To round the meeting off, think about what you have been learning, and thank others for what you have learnt from them.

TIMINGS

The suggestions above are intended for a group that meets for one and a half to two hours. It would divide its time as follows:

Diary	10 minutes
Coming in	Two activities (10 - 15 minutes each) 20 - 30 minutes
Reflecting	Three questions (10 minutes each) 30 minutes
Going out	Two activities (10 - 15 minutes each) 20 - 30 minutes
Prayer & praise	Your own or from resources book 5 - 15 minutes
In the group	5 minutes
Total	1$^1/_2$ - 2 hours

If your group meets for a shorter length of time, reduce the number of activities, but still make sure there is at least one activity from each section:

Diary	5 - 10 minutes
Coming in	One activity (10 - 15 minutes) 10 - 15 minutes
Reflecting	Two questions (10 minutes each) 20 minutes
Going out	One activity (10 - 15 minutes) 10 - 15 minutes
Prayer & praise	5 - 10 minutes
In the group	5 minutes
Total	50 - 75 minutes

GROUP AGREEMENT

Groups often find it helpful to have an agreement about how they will do things to help them work well. Here is an agreement that one group made. You may decide to do something similar.

Sunday, Monday group

I agree: - to try to come to all the group meetings and be on time

- to share my experience and ideas and listen to others

- not to pass on anything that is shared in the group

- to offer help and support to others in the group.

This group will meet on *Tuesday* from *7.30* to *9.30* at *Jane's house*.

We will take turns to bring biscuits.
Fred needs help with baby-sitting (ring him).
If someone can't come they should let Jane know.
PTO for names and addresses.

1

Me, myself, I

If you have not had a previous meeting to get to know each other and make a group agreement, you may wish to spend time doing that now.

Aim

To think about ourselves as human beings created by God and the responsibilities given to us in our different worlds.

Introduction

This session is designed to help your group to consider the ways in which your faith goes with you as you move between your worlds – home, school, work, etc. It will also help you to think about the difference your faith makes to you in these different worlds.

Coming in

Draw

On a large sheet of paper draw yourself as a stick person, making the picture represent some of your characteristics. Then around your stick person use diagrams or pictures of the different places in which you spend time and draw yourself in those places.

| Office full of bright ideas | Church listen | Happy talkative tubby | Home cook, read, often tired | Shops chat |

Share your picture with the rest of the group. Discuss what your picture says about your worlds and how you feel in them.

Objects

As you look around the room see if you can find a number of objects to represent each of the different 'worlds' or places that you spend time in. (It may be that you will not be able to find everything that you want, but try to be imaginative or simply think about what you would have liked to show to others.) Show and explain your objects to the rest of the group. Describe what you are like in these worlds. If there was something that you would have liked to be able to show then describe it to the rest of the group.

Who am I?

Write the answers to the following questions on a piece of paper (do not put your name on the paper). You may not wish to answer all the questions.

1. Where were you brought up?

2. How do you spend most of your time?

3. Who do you share most time with?

4. Name two things you enjoy doing.

5. Name two different worlds that you move in.

Fold your piece of paper and place it in a container in the middle of the group together with everyone else's. One person take out one piece of paper at random and read out the answers. Then everyone try to guess whose paper it is. When you find out, that person takes another piece of paper from the middle, and the process repeats until you have read all the papers.

What, if anything, surprises you about the things that people wrote? What new things have you learnt about them? What does this tell you about people's different worlds?

Split personality?

Draw the outlines of two gingerbread people on a large sheet of paper. Label one 'Sunday' and the other 'Monday'. Write inside 'Sunday' words that describe you at church - your dress, behaviour, feelings, etc. Write inside 'Monday' words that describe the same things wherever you spend most of the rest of the week. Share your sheet with a partner. Talk about any differences between the two sets of words. How do you change between 'Sunday' and

'Monday'? What causes those changes? How do you feel about those changes?

Reflecting

Passages

Listen to the passages being read. Which phrases particularly stick in your mind? If you have trouble remembering all that you have heard, look at the passages again.

Psalm 8:1-9

1 O LORD, our Sovereign,
    how majestic is your name in all
        the earth!

You have set your glory above the
        heavens.
2   Out of the mouths of babes and
        infants
    you have founded a bulwark
        because of your foes,
    to silence the enemy and the
        avenger.

3 When I look at your heavens, the
        work of your fingers,
    the moon and the stars that
        you have established;
4 what are human beings that
        you are mindful of them,
    mortals that you care for them?

5 Yet you have made them a little
        lower than God,
    and crowned them with glory
        and honour.

6 You have given them dominion
        over the works of your
        hands;
    you have put all things under
        their feet,
7   all sheep and oxen,
        and also the beasts of the field,
8   all the birds of the air, and the fish
        of the sea,
    whatever passes along the paths
        of the seas.

9 O LORD, our Sovereign,
    how majestic is your name in all
        the earth!

Matthew 25:14-30

14"For it is as if a man, going on a journey, summoned his slaves and entrusted his property to them; 15to one he gave five talents, to another two, to another one, to each according to his ability. Then he went away. 16The one who had received the five talents went off at once and traded with them, and made five more talents. 17In the same way, the one who had the two talents made two more talents. 18But the one who had received the one talent went off and dug a hole in the ground and hid his master's money. 19After a long time the master of the slaves came and settled accounts with them. 20Then the one who had received the five talents came forward, bringing five more talents saying, 'Master, you handed over to me five talents; see, I have made five more talents.' 21His master

Matthew 25:14-30 continued

said to him, 'Well done, good and trustworthy slave; you have been trustworthy in a few things, I will put you in charge of many things; enter into the joy of your master.' ²²And the one with two talents also came forward, saying, 'Master, you handed over to me two talents; see, I have made two more talents.' ²³His master said to him, 'Well done, good and trustworthy slave; you have been trustworthy in a few things, I will put you in charge of many things; enter into the joy of your master.' ²⁴Then the one who had received the one talent also came forward, saying, 'Master, I knew that you were a harsh man, reaping where you did not sow, and gathering where you did not gather seed; ²⁵so I was afraid, and I went and hid your talent in the ground. Here you have what is yours.' ²⁶But his master replied, 'You wicked and lazy slave! You knew, did you, that I reap where I did not sow, and gather where I did not scatter? ²⁷Then you ought to have invested my money with the bankers, and on my return I would have received what was my own with interest. ²⁸So take the talent from him, and give it to the one with the ten talents. ²⁹For to all those who have, more will be given, and they will have an abundance; from those who have nothing, even what they have will be taken. ³⁰As for this worthless slave, throw him into the outer darkness, where there will be weeping and gnashing of teeth.'

1. What sort of picture of being a human being does this part of Psalm 8 give you? In which, if any, of your everyday situations do you feel as if you act or are treated as this sort of person?

2. The Psalm 8 passage talks about God giving us 'dominion' or authority over the world. In which of your everyday situations do you find yourself exercising authority or responsibility? In which situations, if any, do you wish you could have more responsibility or behave more responsibly?

3. Think about situations in your everyday life where you have some kind of responsibility. Then list five things for which you are responsible. You might want to think of things such as your faith, specific skills you have, your family, work responsibilities, etc. Then rate how well you are developing each of these responsibilities from 1 to 10

(1 = not developing at all and withering away, 10 = totally developed to its full potential). Share your list with a partner. What helps you develop in these areas? What makes it hard?

I am responsible for...	How well am I doing? (circle a number)									
Visiting parents	1	2	3	4	5	(6)	7	8	9	10
	1	2	3	4	5	6	7	8	9	10
	1	2	3	4	5	6	7	8	9	10
	1	2	3	4	5	6	7	8	9	10
	1	2	3	4	5	6	7	8	9	10

4. The 'talents' in the passage from Matthew are sometimes understood to represent the faith that God gives to us. Are there times when you identify with the first servant - having lots of faith, and seeing faith grow a great deal? If so, think when this is. Are there other times when you identify with the second - some faith, and seeing it grow a little? When is this? Are there times when you feel like the third servant - having little faith, and keeping it hidden away? What makes you feel like this? How much do you demonstrate your faith in your home, at your work, in your neighbourhood, in the way you relate to the rest of the world?

5. What kinds of creativity do you see in these passages? What opportunities do you have to be creative in the different 'worlds' you move in? It might be that you think your paid

employment (if you have any) helps you to be creative, or it might be that you find your unpaid employment – perhaps activities like cooking and cleaning – creative. Try to think about what it means for you to use the word creative and where you feel most relaxed about being able to bring things together and make different things.

Going out
Talk
Talk with a partner about one situation where you feel afraid or oppressed. What would you like to change or see changed about that situation? Then talk about a situation where you feel at ease or able to function well. You may like to pray together, aloud or in silence, bringing those situations to God.

Role play
Act out with a partner one situation where you feel uncomfortable about showing your faith. Do a role play in which things are different.

Think
Think about all the different 'worlds' you will move in this week. Then think about the passage again. Are there any connections that come to mind between the passage and the coming week? What are they?

Living it
Psalm 8 tells us that God has given dominion over the world to human beings. How does this make you feel? Circle words in the illustration overleaf. Share your reactions with a partner. Then think together about how this should affect the way in which we live as individuals and collectively. Try to think about this next week as you go about your daily life.

How did it go?

Invite people to say one thing they have enjoyed about the meeting.

Individuals

This week keep a record of the different 'worlds' and situations in which you find yourself. What signs of God do you find in those different places? What difference does your faith make in each of those places? As you keep your record each day offer the things you record to God.

During the week read a portion of the Bible passages each day and think about what God might want to say to you in each of the different worlds in which you might find yourself.

2

The whole world in whose hands?

Love It—
It's the Only
One We've
Got!

Aim

To think about how God intended the world to be and our part in the coming of God's Kingdom (the place where God is in charge).

Introduction

Many people seem unwilling to care for the world that God gave us. Others work for change whether through recycling their waste, or lobbying governments and industry. This session is designed to help you to think about the world as God meant it to be and to consider what you can do to make this picture more of a reality.

Diary

Share what has happened in the past week in your own words.

Coming in

A *wish*

If you had a wish that could change the world, what would it be? Do not be too general (eg 'world peace'), but think about specific situations which you would like to see change. Share your wish with the group.

What, if anything, can you think of that you might be able to do to help your wish to come true?

Creativity

God expects the world to be a place where people are creative, not destructive. Think about what you mean by the word creative. Share this with a partner and then tell them about one creative thing you have done this week.

Following this share one creative thing you have seen or heard of someone else doing this week. What does this tell you about opportunities for being creative in God's world?

Collage

As a whole group use headlines and pictures out of newspapers and magazines to make two collages about the world and events that have taken place. One of the collages should be headed 'Good news', the other headed 'Bad news'.

When you have completed the collages spend a few minutes considering them and then discuss together as a whole group what they tell you about God's world and how human beings treat it.

Reflecting

Passages

Listen to the passages as before.

Micah 4:1,3-4

1 In days to come
   the mountains of the Lord's
      house
  shall be established as the highest
     of the mountains,
  and shall be raised up above the
     hills.

3 He shall judge between many
     peoples,
  and shall arbitrate between
     strong nations far away;
  they shall beat their swords into
     plowshares,

and their spears into pruning
     hooks;
nation shall not lift up sword
     against nation,
  neither shall they learn war any
     more;
4 but they shall all sit under their
     own vines and under their
     own fig trees,
  and no one shall make them
     afraid;
  for the mouth of the LORD of
     hosts has spoken.

Luke 4:16-21

16 When he came to Nazareth, where he had been brought up, he went to the synagogue on the sabbath day, as was his custom. He stood up to read, 17and the scroll of the prophet Isaiah was given to him. He unrolled the scroll and found the place where it was written:

18 "The Spirit of the Lord is upon
     me,
  because he has anointed me
    to bring good news to the
     poor.

He has sent me to proclaim release
    to the captives
and recovery of sight to the
    blind,
to let the oppressed go free,
19 to proclaim the year of the Lord's
    favour."

20 And he rolled up the scroll, gave it back to the attendant, and sat down. The eyes of all in the synagogue were fixed on him. 21Then he began to say to them, "Today this scripture has been fulfilled in your hearing."

1. Go through the passages and mark with a cross the points in the passages where you think the world is not like this at present. Choose one which you could do something about. Share your thoughts with a partner.

2. Who do you think are the 'lame', the 'driven away', the 'afflicted' today? What connections can you see between your situations and theirs?

3. Which of Jesus' statements in verses 18 and 19 is most important to your life? Why is this? Which of these statements do you think the world needs most? Why?

4. These passages paint a picture of the world as God would have it. What do these passages say to you about the world today? Draw a picture or make a model to show your dream of how the world could be.

Going out

You and the world

What effect does the way you spend most of your time have on the rest of the world? Draw or write on two halves of a piece of paper your creative effects and your destructive effects.

I would if...

What are some of the things that make you say 'I would if...' or 'I would except...', eg 'I would recycle my rubbish if the recycling bank was nearer', or 'I would use ecologically sound washing powder except it doesn't get clothes clean'. Choose one that you could actually do something about this week, and plan to do it. Alternatively you might decide it would be right for you to join a particular organisation where you could support or work with others who are concerned about a particular environmental issue. Again plan actually to join this organisation this week. Share your decision and plan with a partner or with the whole group.

Room to improve?

How do you think going to church and reading the Bible should affect what we think about the world and its problems? Try to be as practical as you can with your answer.

Being oppressed

Reflect on the last week and what you have done. Try and make a list of the most important activities with which you have been involved. Then think about whether these things have made you feel free as a person or 'oppressed'. How do you feel about having to do things which make you feel less than free? Explain your answers.

Destructive actions oppress people

Take a large map of the world (preferably a Peter's projection one) and ask group members to put a lighted night light or small candle on places in the world where people are 'oppressed'. It might be that there are certain people and places that individuals are concerned about and they might wish briefly to tell the rest of the group about these. Think about what it would mean for the 'oppressed' of today's world to be free.

In the group

Invite people to name something that they have learnt from someone else in the group this week.

Individuals

This week record instances which contrast the world as it is and how you think it should be. Offer those situations to God.

Read a portion of the Bible passages each day and think about what God might want to say to you in the wider world and your contacts with it.

3

Off to work we go?

Aim

To understand how our work, paid, voluntary and in the home, involves us in God's world and to think about working in a responsible, creative way.

Introduction

No matter what situation you are in you will spend the hours of the day doing something: in paid or unpaid employment, possibly looking after the home and children, or at school or college. This session is designed to help you see that no matter what you do, your life touches God's creation, the world itself and the people in it, and that this brings with it a responsibility to work for change.

Diary

Share things that have happened this last week which show how the world is (rather than how it ought to be).

Coming in

Your work

Take a few minutes to think about how you spend your day. How do you think this affects God's world and God's people? What would you describe as your main work? (Paid/unpaid, activity most time spent on, etc.) Why do you do it? With whom, if anyone, do you work? How do you feel about those people or the lack of people? Share your answers with a partner. Then continue to talk about how you both feel about what you spend most of your time doing. What do you gain from it? What do others gain from it? How do you imagine God feels about it? Finally, share your discussions briefly with the whole group.

Acting

With a partner act out a scene from your day. Act out one thing that you enjoy about it. Then act a scene of one thing you do not enjoy about it. Finally join with another pair and discuss what you have learned from each other's scenes.

Rating

How creative is the way in which you spend your day? What if anything do you do that makes the world a better place? Fill in the chart overleaf and discuss it with the group.

ACTIVITY	IS IT CREATIVE?	DOES IT MAKE WORLD: BETTER, THE SAME OR WORSE?	WHY?

Choice

Draw yourself in the middle of a piece of paper and then illustrate all the forces that brought you to where you are at this stage in your life.

Then show and describe this illustration to a partner. Share with them how much choice you have in the way that you spend your day and what led to you spending your time in this way. How do you feel about this? What would you change if you could? Are there other things that you might want to do but cannot for some reason? Explain your answers.

Reflecting

Passages

Listen to these passages being read as before.

Psalm 104:14-17

14 *You cause the grass to grow for the cattle,*
and plants for people to use,
to bring forth food from the earth,
15 *and wine to gladden the human heart*
oil to make the face shine,
and bread to strengthen the

human heart.
16 *The trees of the LORD are watered abundantly,*
the cedars of Lebanon that he planted.
17 *In them the birds build their nests;*
the stork has its home in the fir trees.

Colossians 3:22-4:1

22*Slaves, obey your earthly masters in everything, not only while being watched and in order to please them, but wholeheartedly, fearing the Lord.* 23*Whatever your task, put yourselves into it, as done for the Lord and not for your masters,* 24*since you know that from the Lord you will receive* the inheritance as your reward; you serve the Lord Christ.* 25*For the wrongdoer will be paid back for whatever wrong has been done, and there is no partiality.*

4 1*Masters, treat your slaves justly and fairly, for you know that you also have a Master in heaven.*

(The writer is not condoning slavery. He is talking to all those who have to obey other people's orders.)

1. Where are you in charge and where are you powerless? How do you feel about situations and roles? What, if anything, would you like to change about them? Why do you answer as you do?

2. Does the passage from Colossians say anything about your situation at work or at home? Discuss this in pairs.

3. The psalm above is written in terms of agricultural work and the natural world. Write a psalm or poem similar to this, but about the sort of work that you do. Write about what you do and how God makes it go well; what your part in the work is and what God's part is. Also express your feelings about this balance. Read your psalm or poem to the group.

4. Place a chair in the middle of the group. This chair is to represent a figure of authority. Ask each member of the group to place an object or objects on this chair which would represent the idealised quality of this person for them. Then, when everyone has placed what they want to on the chair and explained why they have put it there, discuss the activity in the group and how it makes you feel, and what it tells you about the ideal qualities of someone in authority.

Going out

Harvest

What is the 'fruit' or product of your work? Draw or describe something of your work. It would be good if you could bring the thing that you have illustrated to the celebration at the end of this course as a 'harvest offering' from your work.

Faith

In what ways does your faith make a difference to the way that you do and think about your work? What difference does it make to the way you relate to any people you work with? Make a list of these differences, then make a list of other differences you would like your faith to make. What would need to happen to make these things happen?

Doing what must be done

If you are in paid employment or not, what could you do to be creative for yourself and for others?

Advert

Write an advert for your ideal job. Does it exist? If so, would you, could you go for it? Why or why not? If it does not exist, what is the nearest job you can think of to this ideal? How much of this is just dreaming and how much could become reality?

In the group

Name something creative that someone has done in the group this week.

Individuals

Each day this week make a note of one satisfying and one unsatisfying thing that has happened. Offer these things to God.

Read a portion of the Bible passages each day and think about what God might want to say to you in your work.

4

Home sweet family?

Aim

To think about your family and/or friends and how you are creative
and responsible with them.

Introduction

Family is experienced in many different ways today. Some people
live in a small, nuclear family, some in an extended family of several
generations of relatives and friends. Some families have just one
parent, others are the result of combining different families. Some
people have experienced the break-up of a close family grouping

and for some the idea of a close family is an impossible or even undesirable dream. Nonetheless most people feel as if they are part of some kind of network of friends. In fact some people feel that their friends and neighbours are their 'family'.

This session is designed to help you to think about what family and friends are today and how you relate to them.

Diary

Share the record of satisfying and unsatisfying things that happened last week.

Coming in

Your family

What do you think of when someone talks to you about your 'family' and your 'home'? Describe those whom you think of as your family whether they are 'real relatives' or those who have become your family. Then describe the place that you think of as home - this might be where you actually live now or the place that you consider to be home. Share your descriptions with a partner.

Human sculpture

If you have a group of more than six people break into fours or fives. In each group each person should use the other members of their group (and chairs when they run out of people) to make a human sculpture of those with whom you live, or your family, or those whom you have described as your family. Use physical space to represent the closeness of relationships between these people.

When each group member has had a turn, discuss in your small groups what similarities and differences there were in the sculptures. What can be learned from the sculptures? Try to come up with one sentence to summarise your group's findings and share this with the whole group.

Childhood

We all carry things with us from our early years. Some of these things are positive and some negative. Think about the positive and negative things that you carry with you from your childhood and how they affect you now. (These thoughts are just for you, so be as honest as you can. You need only share what you want.)

As you think about your early years, try to describe how faith was or was not expressed in your home when you were a child. What effect has this had on your faith as a adult? How is faith shared in your home now? What symbols of faith are there in the place in which you live, eg a Bible? From where or from whom did they come? Share you answers to these questions with the group.

Think about those people who are of a younger generation than you, particularly small children, with whom you have any sort of involvement. What relationships do you have with them, in what situations? What do you think you might be giving to these people? What are you getting from your relationship with them?

Reflecting

Passages

Listen to these passages in the same way as before.

Deuteronomy 11:18-21

18You shall put these words of mine in your heart and soul, and you shall bind them as a sign on your hand, and fix them as an emblem on your forehead. 19Teach them to your children, talking about them when you are at home and when you are away, when you lie down and when you rise. 20Write them on the doorposts of your house and on your gates, 21so that your days and the days of your children may be multiplied in the land that the Lord swore to your ancestors to give them, as long as the heavens are above the earth.

2 Timothy 1:5-7

⁵I am reminded of your sincere faith, a faith that lived first in your grandmother Lois and your mother Eunice and now, I am sure, lives in you. ⁶For this reason I remind you to rekindle the gift of God that is within you through the laying on of my hands; ⁷for God did not give us a spirit of cowardice, but rather a spirit of power and of love and of self-discipline.

2 Timothy 3:14-17

¹⁴But as for you, continue in what you have learned and firmly believed, knowing from whom you learned it, ¹⁵and how from childhood you have known the sacred writings that are able to instruct you for salvation through faith in Christ Jesus. ¹⁶All scripture is inspired by God and is useful for teaching, for reproof, for correction, and for training in righteousness, ¹⁷so that everyone who belongs to God may be proficient, equipped for every good work.

The Old Testament passage comes at the end of a section in which Moses has been showing how the Ten Commandments affect every day life for the Israelites.

1. Why do you think the Israelites were told to do these things in these ways? How, if at all, was faith passed on to you from your family? What are you now doing to pass faith on in your family?

2. In the group, brainstorm all the ways group members learn about their faith, and write them up. With two colours mark the ones that usually happen on Sunday and the ones that usually happen on a weekday.

3. How do you react to 2 Timothy 3:16-17? Do you feel that scripture helps equip you for good works? If so, what 'good works' do you feel equipped for? How do you feel these might show your faith to others?

4. What does God's power mean in your life and the place in which you live? What might it mean to have a spirit of power, love, and self-discipline in your home or neighbourhood?

Going out

Symbols

Create a symbol that you can use in your home to remind you of some aspect of your faith. Ask everyone to explain the significance of their symbol and to put it in the centre of the group. Then in a time of silence focus on these symbols. Gradually, silently or aloud, use these symbols as the focus for a time of praise and prayer, giving thanks to God for all you have been given, and asking God for help to live as he would want you to.

List

As a whole group or in pairs discuss what things in your homes encourage faith in those who live there and those who visit. What things might discourage faith?

Again in the whole group or in pairs, think of how to encourage and help other families.

Creative

How are you, or could you be, creative at home or with your friends? Discuss your answers with a partner or in the whole group.

Learning from experience

All of us have had good and bad experiences of our 'family' and friends. Make a drawing that expresses a good experience and one that expresses a bad one. What did you learn from each of these experiences? How did you learn from both experiences? What differencies, if any, were there in the way you learnt?

In the group

Say what other people in the group have done to encourage you and show you they care.

Individuals

During the week read a portion of the Bible passages each day and think about what God might want to say to you in your home, or with your friends. Record it if you wish.

5

Everybody needs good neighbours

Aim

To consider what it means to live out your faith in the community.

Introduction

A faith considered on Sunday and ignored on Monday is of very little use. This session will help you to think about practical ways to help in your local community.

Diary

Share with a partner the record you have kept during the last week.

Coming in

Draw

Draw your neighbourhood and the people you know in it. Draw the links, if any, that exist between those people. Use different colours to indicate the different sort of links that people have. Make especial note of those links where one person cares for the other in some way.

Discuss the drawings together. What do they tell you about the neighbourhoods in which you live and the people in them?

Describe

How would you describe communities or neighbourhoods in modern society? Think about all that you know about people in your community. How would you describe them? How do you think they would describe you? How do you feel about your community? How happy are you to be involved in it? What makes you feel that way?

Continuum

Place yourself along an imaginary line drawn through the middle of the room, where one end stands for a very close community and the other for a community where people do not know each other and do not connect at all, at the appropriate point to describe your community. Talk to others who are standing near you, then to people far away from you about being in that place.

Think about whether you all have the same perception of your community if you live in the same area. Or consider what it might be about your community that makes it close or more distant. How would you like your community to be? What might you be able to do to make it more as you think it should be?

Collage

Use the picture you drew of your community or use pictures or words from newspapers, magazines, etc to make a collage of your community. Then add things to represent signs of faith in your community.

Why have you illustrated it in the way that you have? What are you trying to say about it? Is there anything that you would like to change about your community? Why?

Reflecting

Passages

Listen to these passages as before.

Ruth 2:8-13,15-16

8Then Boaz said to Ruth, "Now listen, my daughter, do not go to glean in another field or leave this one, but keep close to my young women. 9Keep your eyes on the field that is being reaped, and follow behind them. I have ordered the young men not to bother you. If you get thirsty, go to the vessels and drink from what the young men have drawn." 10Then she fell prostrate, with her face to the ground, and said to him, "Why have I found favour in your sight, that you should take notice of me, when I am a foreigner?" 11But Boaz answered her, "All that you have done for your mother-in-law since the death of your husband has been fully told me, and how you left your father and mother and your native land and came to a people that you did not know before. 12May the LORD reward you for your deeds, and may you have a full reward from the LORD, the God of Israel, under whose wings you have come for refuge!" 13Then she said, "May I continue to find favour in your sight, my lord, for you have comforted me and spoken kindly to your servant, even though I am not one of your servants."

15When she got up to glean, Boaz instructed his young men, "Let her glean even among the standing sheaves, and do not reproach her. 16You must also pull out some handfuls for her from the bundles, and leave them for her to glean, and do not rebuke her."

Matthew 5: 43-48

43"You have heard that it is said, 'You shall love your neighbour and hate your enemy.' 44But I say to you, Love your enemies and pray for those who persecute you, 45so that you may be children of your Father in heaven; for he makes his sun rise on the evil and on the good, and sends rain on the righteous and on the unrighteous. 46For if you love those who love you, what reward do you have? Do not even the tax collectors do the same? 47And if you greet only your brothers and sisters, what more are you doing than others? Do not even the Gentiles do the same? 48Be perfect, therefore, as your heavenly Father is perfect."

1. What picture of caring for each other do you gain from the Ruth passage? How relevant is the idea of caring for each other today? Who do you think of when someone speaks to you of your neighbours? Do you think that people's ideas of caring for others have changed in recent years? What makes you think as you do?

2. What structures for caring are there in your community? What gaps are there? How could those gaps be filled? How do they compare with the structures outlined in the passages? Discuss your answers in pairs and in the group.

3. How are women and immigrants regarded and treated in your community? How content are you with the way in which they are treated? Do you think that there are changes that ought to be made? What sort of changes would you wish these to be? How could they come about, and what might your part in that be?

4. How realistic and possible is the Matthew passage? How much is it like your life and your relationships with your neighbours? What would need to happen in your neighbourhood for people to treat each other more like this? How could you help see this come about?

Going out

Time

Name one person you could give some time to in your community this week. What might you be able to do? Do you think that they would like you to do this? Alternatively, think of an organisation in your community that helps local people and which you could join or give time to this week.

Those who beg

In many parts of the country today we see people begging for money. How do you react to this? What do you do when you are approached? What might you or your community be able to do to change the plight of those who are in need in your community?

Families

In your area and in your family what is the tradition of looking after each other? Make a body sculpture to picture this. Then stop for a moment and see what this is saying to you. Now manipulate the sculpture to show what would have to happen in your community to make it measure up to the way in which Ruth cared for Naomi and Boaz for Ruth. What, if anything, do you think should be done to bring the two more in line? Describe this to your neighbour in the group.

Perfect neighbours

Write a poem or a piece of prose about your perfect community. Try to describe what it would be like and how it would function. If you feel able, read it aloud in the group. What makes it perfect for you? How does it measure up to your actual community? What, if anything, can you do to help to bring it about where you are? Will you do it?

In the group

Say what you have decided to do to help care for the community.

Individuals

This week keep a record of signs which show that disadvantaged people or people with disabilities are being cared for.

Read a portion of the Bible passage each day and think about what God might want to say to you in your community.

6

The saints go marching out

Aim

To consider how we can live out our faith in all situations as individuals, groups and the church.

Introduction

In the early Christian church, the word 'saints' was commonly used of all believers in Christ. All Saints' Day is a time for us to remember that we are all saints as we live and work to bring about God's kingdom, no matter how we do this. This session is designed to help us realise that we are all saints and to help us think what it means to be a saint now and in the past.

Diary

Share with a partner the things you noticed last week.

Coming in

Draw

Draw a picture of your local community of saints (your church). It doesn't matter how long you have been there. Try to draw it as it was (or you imagine it to have been) five years ago and its relation to the local community. Then draw it now. Draw it as you think it might be in five years time and then finally draw what would need to happen for it to become a new creation - more strongly related to the local community, affecting and being affected by it.

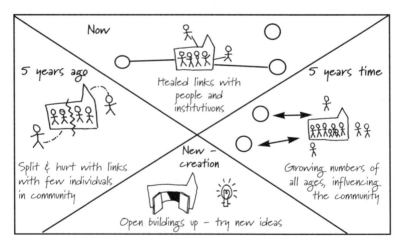

Discuss your illustration with a partner and then think together about the part that you might each have to play in bringing about a new creation in your church(es).

Application

Write a letter of application to be a saint. What qualities do you think you have that fit you for being a saint and what are the qualities which you think you need some help with?

Write a job description for the patron saint that you are applying to be and then add any training needs that you think you have. Share these with a partner.

Chart

Chart, map or graph your life up to this point, particularly marking points of significant change. Then map where you think your life is going, and changes that you hope will occur. Share your map with a partner and think about any similarities in your maps and any differences. Can you learn anything from these concerning the way in which God's 'saints' live their lives? Their hopes and aspirations? Failures and fears? Alternatively do this same exercise but mapping or graphing the life of your church.

Blessing?

In what ways is your church a blessing to your community? Try to think of practical examples of this. Then think about ways in which it might become more of a blessing. Share your answers with the group.

Reflecting

Passages

Listen to these passages in the usual way.

Genesis 12:1-3

¹Now the LORD said to Abram, "Go from your country and your kindred and your father's house to the land that I will show you. ²I will make of you a great nation, and I will bless you, and make your name great, so that you will be a blessing. ³I will bless those who bless you, and the one who curses you I will curse; and in you all the families of the earth shall be blessed."

2 Corinthians 5:14-17

¹⁴For the love of Christ urges us on, because we are convinced that one has died for all; therefore all have died. ¹⁵And he died for all, so that those who live might live no longer for themselves, but for him who died and was raised for them.
¹⁶From now on, therefore, we

2 Corinthians 5:14-17 continued

regard no one from a human point of view; even though we once knew Christ from a human point of view, we know him no longer in that way.

[17]So if anyone is in Christ, there is a new creation; everything old has passed away; see, everything has become new!

1. What do you think it means when God says to Abram that all the people on earth will be blessed through him? How do you think the earth and its peoples are 'blessed' through you? Through your church? Recall those in or outside the church who have been a blessing to you.

2. Do a role play with the group in which each person plays the part of someone in the world community – eg an elderly person, a child, a homeless person, a person in a war zone. Each person should say in what way the church is, or could be, a blessing to him or her.

3. Both passages express the idea of having a relationship with God or of people knowing Christ. In what ways do you feel that you know God? In what ways do you feel that you would like to know God better? How do you think this might come about?

4. The letter to the Corinthians speaks of Christ's love compelling us. Another way of expressing this is that Christ's love 'controls us' (NREB). In what ways, if any, do you experience God's love compelling or controlling you and your church?

5. What, if anything, makes God's love and concern real to you? What might make it real to others? How can you be involved in this?

Going out

Prepare

As a whole group prepare a visual, non-verbal offering for the

Sunday celebration which will mark the end of this course. Everyone in the group should contribute something to it. It should express something of what you have learnt and experienced doing this course together.

Think back over the course. What is the most important thing that you have learnt? Write it on a piece of paper or make a model or draw a picture to illustrate it. Then during the service take it up to the front or put it in the offertory. During the time of intercession give thanks for all that you have learnt and ask God's help to live as God would want.

Discuss together what you think it means to live out the faith that you learn about in church on Sunday in whatever you do on a Monday. How can the memory of this group and the people in it help you to live your faith each day? Is there anything that you might be able to agree to do to help each other even if the group will not meet again in the same way? Will you do this?

Try to think of some new action that you will take as a result of this course. It might be that this is something obviously practical, or that it is to pray for each other, etc. But whatever it might be, however big or small, try to come up with one definite outcome of the course for you. Share this with a neighbour and then as a whole group commit yourselves to doing these things.

In the group
Listen to the group name things that people have contributed to the group.

Individuals
Each morning ask God to show you what you can do in your worlds to help God's kingdom come.

Each evening offer to God what you have been able to do.